LEVEL 2 READER

W9-BKM-225

Pet Babies

by
Joan Emerson

Scholastic Inc.

PHOTO CREDITS:

Photos ©: cover: Mark Taylor/Warren Photographic; cover background: Andrew_
Howe/iStockphoto; back cover: oscarshost/iStockphoto; 1: Mark Taylor/Warren
Photographic; 1 background: Andrew_Howe/iStockphoto; 2-3 background and
throughout: JoyTasa/Thinkstock; 3: anurakpong/iStockphoto; 4 dog tag and
throughout: Elisabeth Burrell/Dreamstime; 4 metal on dog tag and throughout:
CG Textures; 4 plaid blanket and throughout: Choreograph/iStockphoto; 5: Jim
Craigmyle/Corbis Images; 6: Smitt/iStockphoto; 9: Herbert Spichtinger/Media Bakery;
10: Iuliia Gatcko/Shutterstock, Inc.; 13: Zigmund Leszczynski/Animals Animals; 14:
oscarshost/iStockphoto; 17: Olga Itina/Dreamstime; 18: Paul Freed/Animals Animals;
21: M. Watson/Animals Animals; 22: Photos77777/Dreamstime; 25: Rober Maier/
Animals Animals; 26: luckypic/Shutterstock, Inc.; 29: Eugenesergeev/Dreamstime; 30:
Marie-Ann Daloia/123RF.

No part of this publication may be reproduced, stored in a retrieval system, or
transmitted in any form or by any means, electronic, mechanical, photocopying,
recording, or otherwise, without written permission of the publisher. For information
regarding permission, write to Scholastic Inc., Attention: Permissions Department, 557
Broadway, New York, NY 10012.

ISBN 978-1-338-03822-4

Copyright © 2016 by Scholastic Inc.
All rights reserved. Published by Scholastic Inc., *Publishers since 1920.* SCHOLASTIC and
associated logos are trademarks and/or registered trademarks of Scholastic Inc.

The publisher does not have any control over and does not assume any responsibility
for author or third-party websites or their content.

10 9 8 7 6 5 4 3 2 1   16 17 18 19 20 21

Printed in China   68
First printing, September 2016

Book design by Marissa Asuncion
Photo Editor: Emily Teresa

Introduction

Everyone has seen pet dogs and cats in the house, but did you know some people have alpacas or boa constrictors as pets? Owning a pet is a very big responsibility, and caring for a baby pet can be even tougher! No matter the animal, pet babies need food, water, and lots of love. Turn the page to meet some of the cutest pet babies around.

Dog

Dogs are some of the most popular pets in the United States. Some dogs are as big as ponies, and others are as small as guinea pigs. There are lots of differences in kinds of dogs, but they all start off the same way—as puppies! Puppies are born blind and deaf, but soon they'll be able to see and hear much better than humans. Puppies need lots of exercise, food, and care, so they can grow up strong and healthy.

There are 339 **breeds** of dogs, and no two look exactly the same.

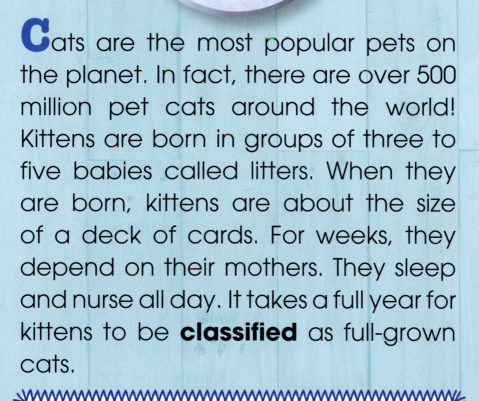

Cat

Cats are the most popular pets on the planet. In fact, there are over 500 million pet cats around the world! Kittens are born in groups of three to five babies called litters. When they are born, kittens are about the size of a deck of cards. For weeks, they depend on their mothers. They sleep and nurse all day. It takes a full year for kittens to be **classified** as full-grown cats.

Cats have the incredible ability to sense a human's mood.

Pig

A dog. A cat. A pig? That's right, some people have pigs as pets! Piglets are cute and cuddly. They usually weigh about two-and-a-half pounds when they are born. But they can grow to over two hundred pounds as adults. Pigs love to snuggle and get their bellies scratched. And they are very smart. They can even learn to open doors! Pet pigs need a lot of room, so make sure you have enough space before you get one!

Potbellied pigs can respond to their names and be taught simple tricks.

Chinchilla

Chinchillas are part of the rodent family, and they are about the size of squirrels. Originally from the mountains of South America, they can jump as high as six feet. Chinchillas are extra-cuddly pets because they have the softest fur in all of the animal kingdom! A baby chinchilla, called a kit, is born with all its soft fur and weighs less than one pound.

Chinchillas have razor-sharp teeth that never stop growing.

Gecko

Geckos are a type of lizard. Geckos usually lay two eggs at a time. Newborn geckos are called hatchlings. They are born with super skills that many other animals do not have. Some geckos have sticky footpads so they can walk on the ceiling! Others use **camouflage** to blend into their surroundings. And, if a **predator** attacks a gecko's tail, it can even shed it and grow a new one. These skills make geckos very interesting pets!

Just like dogs, geckos wag their tails when they get excited!

Alpaca

Alpacas are originally from Peru, but these days, many people in the United States own them as pets. Alpacas are known for their special hair, called fiber. People use it to make blankets, scarves, and coats. The alpaca babies, called cria, are about 10–20 pounds at birth. They are born with full coats of fiber. They make good pets because they are friendly and can follow one-word commands.

Watch out! Alpacas have been known to spit when they get angry.

Horse

Even the tallest horse was once just a foal. When a foal is born, it weighs only 100–200 pounds. That might sound like a lot, but it will grow to be at least ten times that weight! Soon after they are born, foals take their first steps. They can even trot within a few hours. Still, a foal cannot give any rides until it is at least one year old. It needs to grow big and strong before it can carry a rider.

People have kept horses for over 5,500 years!

Boa Constrictor

Mother boa constrictors can give birth to up to sixty babies at a time. A newborn baby boa is usually called a neonate. When it is born, it is only about two feet long. Adult boa constrictors can reach over twelve feet, which means they need very large cages. Pet owners also have to be comfortable around rodents, because boas need to be fed rats, hamsters, or gerbils!

After a boa constrictor eats one big meal, it doesn't have to eat again for weeks!

Rabbit

By the early 1900s, people began breeding rabbits as pets. They make perfect pets because they are small, they like to be cuddled, and they can even perform simple tricks. A mother gives birth to a litter of about thirteen rabbits called kits. That is a big family! The babies live in a nest together for 2–3 weeks. When a group of rabbits lives together like this, it is called a **herd**.

Rabbits are **herbivores**, which means they eat only vegetables and plants.

Parrot

Parrots are common pets in American households. They are easy to care for because they are small and they do not need to be walked. When parrot chicks are born, they have fluffy down. They start growing their colorful feathers when they are about three weeks old. Parrots are smart, too! Many parrots are able to **mimic** human speech. You can teach them words while they are babies, just like with humans!

Parrots have been known to live over eighty years!

Hamster

Hamsters are very popular pets in the United States because they are small, clean, and quite easy to care for. When it is born, a hamster pup is about the length of a paperclip and as light as a dinner fork. Hamsters are **crepuscular**, which means they are most active at dawn and dusk. So you may not want to put your hamster's cage in your bedroom—your pet could wake you up early!

All golden hamsters are believed to be **descendants** of one hamster couple found in 1930!

Goldfish

Freshwater fish are the most popular pet in American households. Goldfish are a type of freshwater fish that have been kept as pets for over two thousand years. A goldfish baby, called a fry, is smaller than an eyelash when it's born! Soon it will grow to be about two to three inches long. A pet goldfish can live more than twenty years.

The biggest goldfish ever found was eighteen inches long!

Sugar Glider

A sugar glider is a member of the **marsupial** family, which includes animals like kangaroos and koalas. They have wings that let them glide through the air, and they can live up to fourteen years. Baby sugar gliders are called joeys. They are about the size of a grain of rice when they are born. If you have a sugar glider as a pet, it may wake you up when it wants to play. That's because sugar gliders stay up all night!

Like other marsupials, mother sugar gliders carry their babies in their stomach pouches.

Turtle

Turtles have been on this planet for over 250 million years. They used to live alongside the dinosaurs, but today they can live right in your bedroom! Freshwater turtles are the most common types of pet turtles. Turtle babies, called hatchlings, are smaller than the palm of your hand and weigh less than an ounce. Turtles start off small, but some species can grow to over two thousand pounds.

Although turtles breathe air, some species can stay underwater for four to five hours at a time!

Glossary

breed: a particular type of plant or animal

camouflage: natural coloring that allows an animal to hide by looking like its surroundings

classify: to put things into groups according to things they have in common

crepuscular: being most active at twilight or when the sun is rising

descendants: a couple's children, or other direct family members in the future

herbivore: an animal that eats only plants

herd: a group of animals that stays together

marsupial: an animal known for the pouch on the mother's belly, where she carries her babies

mimic: to imitate someone else

predator: an animal that hunts other animals for food